To Frav

WORDS OF A SOUL

By

Lisa Fulham

This piece of my soul now belongs to you. I hope it connects to yours.

Stay true to your heart

Lisa Fulham

xxx
x

This piece of my Soul
now belongs to you.   hope
it connects to yours.

Stay true to your
heart

Part 3 - Depths

Part 4 - Love

Foreword

Poetry is an enigma, a rising hope and a spark of passion rolled into one. I'd never thought about writing poetry, but poetry has a knack of working its way into the soul.

This book is a re-mastered and extended version of my poetry book Words of a Season which I felt needed updating to reflect who I am as a poet, writer and broken soul. Everyone has their own broken pieces they try to hold together every day in life through moments of despair and in blinding moments of love. This book is my homage to my cherished broken pieces.

I have a few thank you's I'd like to make before going any further.

Firstly, I would like to thank Cameron Lincoln. Without his friendship and support I would have never taken the first steps on my journey as a writer and I certainly wouldn't have come as far as I have. This man is a true inspiration and I shall remind him of this and cherish him always x

I would like to thank Paige Thomas who has become such a huge part of my life and even from half the world away she makes me feel loved x

I couldn't talk about poetry without thanking PJ Bayliss. This man was the first poet I interacted with on social media. He is my benchmark, the poet I aspire to be even half as good as, he is a friend.

Part 1 – Ice

The cold burns, sets you alight

Siawords

Lisa xxxx

The Prince of the Forest

His heart was cold and empty until *she* came along

And scorched him with her burning passion

While the trees shivered in delight

At witnessing the love they shared

Together they were two snow angels side by side

A love mirrored by the surrounding white blanket

They wandered hand in hand

Dreaming of their life together

Following the footsteps

Of those who had walked the path of love before them

Creating fresh ones of their own for those who followed
behind

Coming to a fork in the road

They discovered a path never before explored

And embarked on a new journey

One of Life, Love and Passion

So delighted with their new direction

They missed the fox stalking the snowy hilltop

Ready pounce and devour

The prince of the forest was still and patient

Waiting until passion roared within him

Before he gave chase

As the lovers walked on

The snows beauty

Hid the dirt which lay underfoot

They passed a barbed wire fence

Twisted and cruel

Yet the snow still fell

Adorning it with beauty

Love as pure as snow

Does not discriminate who it bestows itself upon

They came to a clearing with a mighty pond

In the middle stood the fox

He had come to reclaim *his* snow angel

The fox's howl pierced the silence

Causing a snow storm to whirl around his love

As she returned to the one who truly held her heart

The prince of the forest

A tortured scream rang out

As the angel and fox fell beneath the ice surface

The scream ripped from his soul

The cracks in the ice were his reminder

Of the depths of despair which linger beneath the surface

Of Winter, of Love, of Life

The System Shall Fall

Rubble cuts underfoot

Silence deafens the few who survived

As the backbone of our society lays in ruins before us

How often did people disregard the small white piece of card?

A symbol of democracy unworthy of their attention

The system is already flawed

Their default excuse for none action

But a flawed system gives hope

It's a starting point filled with things we cannot allow

Where we can build a new system

Without the flaws we've lived with for so long

We were warned the system shall fall

A warning many did not heed

Democracy or Communism

Liberal or Democrat

Every side has been fought

Each party wears their own scars of victory and defeat

But they *were* fought for

With blood and loss and hate

By men, women and children

Before our lands become wasteland

Before all sides lose this race

Put *your* vote into the mix

Make sure there's a box

Which bears your cross

<u>December</u>

This is my December

My winter, my storm

I am without

Your warmth, your love

The winds of my sorrow

Blow through my empty heart

A barren place

You left behind

Every day my mind projects

A silent movie

Focused on everything I've lost

Everything you took

I am forever frozen

Inside my own December

My continued ending

Without the promise of a new beginning

This. Is my. December

<u>Flash Poetry</u>

Be my spring bloom

Breathe new life

Into my heart

Show me how to live

I want to be your snowdrop

A burst of colour

Bringing you joy

Melt my fears

As I reach

For the brightest star

The sun

Your love

The Bloom of Winter

She was a vision

Purer than the snow

And as delicate as a snowflake

Her cheeks shone pink

Against her alabaster skin

And as I saw her

Kneeling beneath the tree

She made my heart sing

The song was not one filled with joy

She was abstract

Separate from the beautiful forest surrounding her

She outshone its grace

Yet there was something sad

And dispirited about her

Her innocence was in her every curve

Her stature

Her sorrow

She never moved from her state of prayer

Her white rosemary beads

Shone in the winter sun

And although her mouth appeared not to move

A mist rose from her lips

She was an angel

Yet she was broken

Surrounded in winter whites

While her heart was breaking

As I moved closer

I could hear her litany prayer

"My winter is never ending

Without my love by my side

Please allow our springtime

Turn my white rose crimson

And melt the ice of separation"

The winter angel

Was out of season

Springtime was her magic

The world to her eyes was wrong

Every white rose I've seen since I heard her prayer

I have hoped it turns crimson

For the love she missed

Through the ice and snow

Flash Poetry

Expression can be hard to achieve

Definition

More so

When the West winds blow

Through the hollow oak

Where will our minds nest?

When will we find

Contentment

The Snowflake

The beauty of a snowflake is endless

Each one unique

Lasting forever in a wish

Catch one and feel her grace

As she melts into your soul

The snowflake drifts from the heavens

She is humble, she is pure

She seeks your warm embrace

Despite it meaning her end

Each snowflake is the winter angel's love

Her ice and your fire combined

Will create a pool of love

The snowflake is a timeless beauty

Flash Poetry

The year is slipping by

The air holds

Winters chill

You wrap your arms around me

Become my blanket against the cold

Your love is the fire

Melting the ice encasing my heart

Turning my internal winter

Into a glorious

Never ending

Spring

Part 2 - Darkness

Even in the darkest moments your light shines and guides others. Remember that, always.

Lisa

xxx

The Haunted Asylum

She was jovial today

Almost giddy

Her skin tingled with excitement

She knew she shouldn't be here

They had chased her away before

But there was something arousing

And mythical

About this fanciful place

It sang to her heart

It felt like home

A home she was yet to be accepted into

But one where she longed to be

The people inside those walls

Were the luckiest people

She could ever imagine

She craved to have her own demented screams

Swallowed and absorbed

Amongst those who resided

On the inside of this beautiful fortress

She had once seen some of the people who lived here

They were in the garden

And they wore white jackets

That wrapped their arms around them

They were hugging themselves

She had tried to wrap her own arms around herself

But it wasn't the same

She needed the pretty buckles and straps

Hugging yourself whilst restrained

Could there be a better feeling?

She pondered this question

And remembered the time

She had crept around the back of the building

Where there were windows close to the floor

And she could see down into the basement

They kept a special bed there

With cuffs at the top and bottom

With cranks at one end

She'd watched from the window

As a woman was dragged into the room

Kicking and screaming

Her dirty linen nightgown torn

And flailing around her ankles

Two men hauled her onto the bed

And yanked her hands above her head

In the fight to secure the woman

Her nightgown had risen

To the top of her thighs

It made her quiver in excitement

To bear witness to such a thing

And she wondered what would happen next

The woman's legs were pulled apart by rough hands

Her ankles were secured also

The woman was spread open for all to see

Her skin glistened in the moonlight

While she screamed

Cried and sobbed

Pleading the men to stop

That's when it began

The cranks were turned

Her body went taut

The woman's piercing scream

Pulled at her heart

She wanted

No

She needed that

Held down

Stretched out

Spread open

Rage

Lust

And longing

Rushed through her body

That was then

This is now

What was captivating her in this moment

Were the shadows created by the lights

Glowing from the small windows

The bars adding depth

To the light and darkness

Up the walls and across the floor

As the lights went out one by one

More shadows appeared

And her thoughts turned to the blessed beings

Who had graced the rooms

Of this magical palace

Before death had gifted them eternal darkness

She yearned to feel the remnants of their souls

Passing through her own

To feel the chill of their sorrow

Mixed with hers

She shivered in longing

Her heart breaking

She

Was still on the outside

She began to claw at her own skin

Causing angry red welts to appear

As her nails dragged down her arms

The haunted asylum was her home

She just needed

To find the right key

To the door

The Fog, The Darkness

The fog. The mist. The darkness

They conspire against me

I'm cold. I'm lonely

I ache inside

No arms of comfort surround me

Here my thoughts turn dark and deviant

They twist my words before my eyes

While pictures dance inside my head

Things I should not have seen

Should not have experienced

But they lurk in the darkness

Ready to remind me when times are bleak

There is no comfort from your own thoughts

No escape

Memories haunt us

Our hearts break

Tears fall ungoverned

The parted are at ease

They rest in their sleep

They cannot remember

And they no longer hurt

These times seem so dark

Even the light is blinding

It leaves us without sight

But what is there to see?

Pain. Destruction. Heartbreak

Oh darkness which consumes me

You make me grow weary

I am tired

I am spent

Someone please guide me

Through the darkness

The mist

The fog

Someone please show me the soft glow of life once more

<u>Broken Angel</u>

The broken angel fell from the heavens

Her grace torn apart

Her heart an open wound

She once soared in the heavens

She once basked in glorious light

Her wings have turned raven black

She now hides from those she used to know

The broken angel dared to hope for a love of her own

That hope was crushed

The one she loved belonged to another

Now she covers her face

Her eyes pouring out her sorrow

She cannot fly on broken dreams

She cannot walk laden with sadness

She sits upon her rock of despair

Locked for eternity with the crows

Who squawk at her arrogance

Of ever hoping for a love to call her own

She was an angel

That was her gift of love

Now she is broken

Surrounded by her shattered dreams

An angel no more

Just a broken soul

The Lonely Man on the Canal

They had walked this path a thousand times together

It had always felt too short

Walked alone

It felt like an eternity

Like his heart

The water of the canal was still

Like his soul

It held dark depths

The branches of the overgrown trees reached out to him

Trying to show him there was still life

And it was beautiful

But he turned away from them

And walked on

Further along their beaten path

The old blossom tree created an arch

Like the one they married beneath

His broken heart shattered further

At the memory of her beauty

Under this very tree they had made promises

The word forever had been whispered

But forever had been cut too short

The path had narrowed over time

Now it was only needed for one

The world felt smaller when walking alone

The bridge was where it all started

Their first walk

First kiss

And the 'I do'

Now it was defaced

Not by the graffiti

But by her death

Tear it down

Break it into a thousand pieces

His heart was broken without her

He now and forever will be known as

The Lonely Man on the Canal

Our Beach

I walked along our beach today and the sand felt different underfoot

The grains were coarse

Tiny shards piercing my heart with every step I took

I walked along our beach today

Without your hand within my grasp

My fingertips missed your touch

I walked along our beach today while the tide was out to sea

With no waves to wash away my solitary footprints

I left a trail of loneliness in my wake

I walked along our beach today and the sky felt my sorrow

My pain

My loss

I walked along our beach today and saw the clouds mirror my anger

Turning darker by the minute

Just as my heart does without you

I walked along our beach today and found our special place

The one which held such promise

When it was home to our love

I walked along our beach today with you by my side

I felt you in every step I took

As I know I will each day I am alone

The sand, the tide, the sky

And our special place

Mourned with me

I spread your ashes along our beach today

And there my love is where you'll stay

I'll join you soon

No doubt my love

And we shall forever

Walk along our beach together

<u>The Stalk Her</u>

Her love for him over took her

It seeped from her every pore

Rippled through her

With the force of almighty waves

As if conjured by Titan himself

She dreamt of him when awake

When she slept

He invaded her being

Devouring her essence

She sat in his garden

Surrounded by snow

And contemplated the time old question

Does he love me?

Picking a blood red rose

She began her

He loves me. He loves me not's

So consumed in her question

She did not hear the rose scream in pain

So distracted was she

She had forgotten the rose lived too

As she plucked the last petal

She was given the answer she feared most

He loves me not

The rose was dead

Her heart was dead

And now her love must die too

Encircled by crimson

She made her plan

The first time her love saw her face

It would be the last face he ever saw

With death

They would part

It was as if Death himself whispered in her ear

The melody of his words were her hearts song

He understood her need

Her desire

Her ultimate goal

She knew her love would be sleeping

His room was easy to find in the dark

She had been there before to watch him sleep

His dog made no sound as she approached

He was used to her and her nightly visits

And she always brought him steak

Sliding her bobby pin into the lock

The door popped open with ease

She had greased the hinge on her last visit

Her floor length black gown

Gave the illusion of a ghost

Gliding through the house

The almost silent rustles it made

Added to the ghostly image

Reaching his bedroom

She stopped

The sight of him naked on the white cotton sheets

Made her pulse race

But she remembered the last petal

And its message

Hidden in her pocket sat her silver dagger

She caressed it before pulling it out

Running the blade through her fingers

The moonlight reflected off the polished surface

And danced on the walls

Excitement coursed through her veins

He would finally see her face

And she would make sure

His last heartbeat

Would beat for her

Slowly undressing

Her gown pooled at her feet

Was it ironic?

They should be naked as the day they were born

On the night they would die

Silently she crept up his body

Softly dragging her sex along his manhood

Wishing he was hard

She whispered against his lips

"Wake up my soul mate

Your love is here"

His eyes opened

Fear shining in their dark depths

"I loved you with all my being

How could you not love me back?"

That's when she struck

Plunging the dagger into his heart

She swallowed his pained gasp

With a kiss

Sitting up

She watched the life drain from his eyes

While death bellowed his hollow laugh

A reminder of the next action she must take

Shifting their bodies

She embraced his still warm corpse

And with the same dagger

Slashed both her wrists

Deep

She wanted to feel her love for him

Flow out of her with every beat of her heart

For it to saturate them both

A smile played on her lips

Her parting words to the world

"Together for eternity

Now you will learn to love me"

<u>Night Fears</u>

Waking in the dark

Heart pounding

Mind racing

What was that?

A noise?

Mind scrambles

Clutches at straws

In a twisted way

I want to see

What lies behind

Those closed doors

Pulse still racing

Eyes screwed shut

Why did I wake up?

Turn on the light

A blinding moment

Looking at the clock

Time looking back

Mocking

Sitting in the light

Mind still in the dark

Do I hear the morning lark?

Another night of disturbed sleep

My mind is troubled

When I should be asleep

Flash Poetry

Guilt

I feel it in my bones

Hear it in my voice

An unwanted part of me

Embedded in my soul

I take less than I need

And give more than I have

But it's never enough

To make me feel worthy

Of those who love me

And so my guilt drowns me

Blinding me to my worth

<u>Wedding Day</u>

I woke to the morning lark's song

The sky was clear and blue

Today all my dreams were to come true

We were to be joined in holy matrimony

The dress was hung

All lace and silk

My glowing skin

As white as milk

I prepared myself for you

Every detail with you in mind

My mother fussed

All loving and kind

My hair all curled

Dress fastened tight

My father's eyes teared

At the virginal sight

The horse drawn carriage

Travelled too slow

I wanted to speed towards you

To put our love on show

Flowers filled the church

Every pew adorned with smiling faces

You stood at the alter

Awaiting your bride

Looking noble and princely

My father handed me over to you

With nothing but pride in his heart

That's when you tore my world apart

You ripped your hand from mine

My cheeks became crimson

Like red wine

You turned and walked away from me

No explanation

No reason why

You left my life

So now I cry

Lay on my bed

The one we should have shared

Now I shall forever look upon it

As the place where my heart bled

A bride no longer

Just the shattered mess you left

Wearing a beautiful

Wedding dress

<u>Your Ghost</u>

I remember you

Your touch

Your smell

The way you felt inside my soul

I miss you

Your caress

Your ability to see me

The way you brought me to heights unknown

I yearn for you

The smiles you dragged from me

The giggles you tickled from me

Your replying joy and the promise of more

I crave you

My body betrays me

Clenching at memories

Heating at desires

While longing for your touch

The ghost of our past

Wakes me in the night

Stops me in my tracks

Quickening my pulse

Haunting me

I remember you

But now you're just a ghost

Who knows my secrets

<u>Flash Poetry</u>

Each dawn

Brings new adventure

Bask in the unknown

Never let the depth

Of a puddle

Stop you

From jumping in

With both feet

Splash

In the puddle

Of life

Part 3 - Depths

The depths of our souls is
infinite. We are not meant to
find the bottom. Just swim in
its magnificence.

Lisa xxx

Mother Nature's Anguish

Something has happened to the world

At times when we should bask in the light

The morning offers nothing but darkness

The seasons are out of sync

When there ought to be glorious sunshine

We quiver in the cold

When snowflakes are meant to offer their magic

The trees are in bloom

Even the birds are unsure

When they should be flying south

The axis is broken

Good and evil are no longer counterbalanced

Evil has tipped the scales in its favour

And what of man?

Man is the greatest contributor to this change

Man forgot the importance of the earth and her beauty

Man forgot it was his duty to protect her

He marred her landscape with greed and selfishness

Man created the darkness

That steals our morning light

Timeless and Wise

The weathered and wise tree

Towers over man

As natures symbol of life

Breathing air into the heart of Mother Nature

He sees the seasons come and go

Time and time again

Year after year

Spring offers hope of new beginnings

A farewell to the cold and lonely nights

Summer brings the sun

Its warmth spreading love and happiness

With nights spent around the campfire under the stars

As autumn arrives

The colours of the world change

Amber, Burgundy and inspiration tumble and swirl

New chapters are written

In the never ending story of life

As another year draws to a close

Winter blows through the soul

The cold freezes the hearts

Of those trapped in the darkness of a winter storm

While others curl by the fire

Admiring the winter wonderland

Throughout each change

The tree stands tall

Gaining wisdom from the world around him

Learning from the mistakes of man

The tree is timeless

Hiding his age

Until man is foolish enough to end him

The tree is wise

Weathering the winter

To enjoy all four magical seasons of life

Knowing that without the cold

The warm would not feel so nourishing

Twilight

Neither day

Nor night

Not quite awake

Yet sleep remains out of reach

The sky draws patterns

Colours merge

The industrial scar of life

Mares the landscape

Where it joins the magical sky

Dreams unfulfilled by day

Wait to be dreamt once more

In slumber

All things are possible

But until that time comes

I'll sit and gaze upon an oil painted sky

Some see twilight as the end of the day

Others see it

As the beginning of the night

It's time to let the adventure begin

To let the love of life take hold

To say goodbye to the sun

To pour out your heart to the stars

Because once twilight is over

Comes the promise of night

Allow the moon to shine bright

Deep into your soul

The space between day and night

Is not dead

Is not a void

But is full of all which can come true

If you believe in the magic

It holds

The Storm That Built

The storm has been brewing

The clouds have been gathering

Swirling

Getting bigger and darker than ever before

They're filled with anger and angst

Sorrow and sensitivity

Deviance and demolition

The winds whip my face

The rain stings my eyes

I am battered, bruised and wounded

Yet here I stand on the precipice

Staring into the face of this mighty storm

Neither of us willing to admit defeat

A storm of this magnitude will take a war to conquer

A mere battle will be insignificant

Yet

Here

I

Stand

The un-calm before the storm

Raw Emotion

I sit and allow the tears to fall

There's no reason for them

I'm lucky in so many ways

But my mind plays cruel games

I always wonder why people spend time with me

Do they not see the monster raging inside?

I feel as though my strings have been cut

I'm on the outside

Stuck in my rut

Anxiety is a vicious thing

Causing heart palpitations

Amongst other things

Will I ever feel as though I'm enough?

Will I be the diamond in the rough?

I know I'm not alone in the world

And I need to take my own advice

But my voice is not strong

And I my words to myself come out wrong

Being kind is who I am

Yet sometimes I just want to

Scream and shout

I'm a stubborn coward

I'd rather climb this goddam wall

Alone

Just me

So I can see how far I refused to fall

A fighter is who I am

I'll fight these tears

And their fucking dam

<u>Hurricane</u>

In the eye of the storm

There's silence and calm

As destruction swirls around me

Here in the eye

I find tranquillity

An inner peace

The sky shines bright and blue

Above my head

I know it's only a matter of time

Before the storm swallows me whole

Lifts my feet from the green grass

I see the herculean winds

Swirling ever closer

And I smile at the onslaught

I know will take me

There is no escape

No sanctuary from the beast

As it inches ever closer

I look at what has been uprooted

At what flies within this raging storm

Hope

Peace

Love

Kindness

Life

Friendship

I was expecting

Houses

Cars

Fences

And cows

That's when it hits me

Just before the eye passes over me

Before I am sucked in

This storm was created by me

Born from my swirling thoughts

There is no Land of OZ

No red slippers to click

The good witch

The wicked witch

Both reside in me

I am them and so much more

As my feet lift

I'm carried into the grey winds

Only I can bring this monster to heel

Only I can stop the destruction

Only I can bring about my own rainbow

<u>Lady in the Rain</u>

The lady

As she was known

Appeared each rainfall

People came from far and wide

To see the legend they had heard of

As the first raindrops fell from the sky

She would appear

Her gown trailing along the floor

Kneeling upon the stone steps

She became statuesque

As she raised her face into the deluge

She was defiant

Resolute and strong

It didn't seem to matter how much rain fell

How soaked she became

She simply smiled up to the clouds

Emanating kindness

And although she looked like a stone angel

She appeared soft, gentle

And warmed the hearts of those

Who came to witness her pilgrimage

She was an enigma

An untold story

As the last raindrop touched her face

She would bow her head in gratitude

For what?

No one ever knew

Sodden and see through

Her dress now clung to every curve

She arrived a lady

She left a Greek Goddess

The Lady in the Rain

Contradiction

I am not a contradiction

I am many things at once

I am confident

Yet unsure of myself

I smile

With tears in my eyes

I love myself for who I am

And hate who I can be

I offer my friendship

But fear I will be a disappointment

I like the shadows

While I shine my light on others

I try to guide those who need it

But I am always lost

I am happy and sad

Confident and shy

I am a bow untied

I am a contradiction

The Chapel, the Minster and I

Search inside to find your faith

Love spills from your heart for others

Reflect on your victories

And acknowledge the wars you've triumphed

Faith in the almighty

Can only be found within

Worship the struggles you've overcome

Believe that the ever raging internal war

Will be won

Surrender yourself to joy

Allow it to shine on those you love

Including yourself

Stride through your battlefields in life

Plant your seeds of love

And bask in your own poppy fields

Where each flower is a representation

Of everything you have achieved

Kneel at the Altar of life

Use your spirit

To guide your flock

And prosper

In the currency

Of your faith

In yourself

<u>Part 4 - Love</u>

A heart which has never been broken can never understand the beauty of a heart put back togethe to be whole once more.

Lisa xxx

<u>Flash Poetry</u>

The world is our playground

Spilling over with

Light

And darkness

Climb its monstrous mountains

Swim in its inspiring oceans

Drown

In your own creativity

The Love That Waited

Her soul sighed

As she whispered

His name

Over and over

A mantra

To her love

As he lay in bed

His mind conjured

An image of pure beauty

She didn't have a face

She had a soul

Which sang to his heart

Life had played a cruel trick

So close they had come

To a life together

Only to have it ripped away

As they were left clutching at air

Drowning in their despair

She had packed her bags

Said her goodbyes

And was ready to embark

On an adventure

Of the heart

Her mother's death

Had tore her apart

His service should have been over long ago

But war made him stay

And fight

To protect his homeland

His love

Their freedom

His heart would have to wait

Both were hurting

Both were lost

Their love was covered

Laying in wait

For their return

As the world does

It carried on turning

Time passed

Different lives they'd had to live

In the absence of each other

The years had been kind to her

While he wore his scars of war

In the night they both woke

Their hearts

Their souls

Began their song once more

The search was on

Their love their guiding compass

Both heading north

Feeling the others warmth

The closer they came

Life had been cruel once

But this time

It was their game

Their rules

And neither would stop

Until their reunion

Was complete

Stood on a hillside

Over looking white cliffs

He was a vision to her eyes

The tears came

And as he turned

He was crying too

"I can't believe it's really you"

"Ssshh my love

I came for you"

On that hillside

They stood

Embraced

And watched the sun set

In the morning

They rushed to that same spot

And watched the sun rise

The dawn of the new day

The dawn of their new life

Together

Love waited

Love lasted the test of time

Of distance

Of life

Flash Poetry

Love is not

A date on a calendar

It's not

Defined by time

And cannot be measured

By distance

Love is

All consuming

Throughout

Time

And over

Immeasurable miles

The Test of Time

The grains of time flow too fast

Yet here I stand

Stationary

People fly by in a flurry

Rushing here and there

Yet here I stand

Stationary

I aim for progression

Whilst trying to fight the feeling of retreat

Yet here I stand

Stationary

Stuck whilst the world passes by

Screaming into the wind while being silent

Yet here I stand

Stationary

And here I'll stay

Until I can move my feet

Until my screams are no longer silent

Until the day I no longer stand here

Stationary

<u>Friend</u>

Lost and broken

Cold and alone

I thought I'd received

All the gifts life had to offer me

I never saw you coming

I didn't foresee this happening

Into my life you crept

Under my hearts radar

And brought with you

Light

Learning new things about myself

From stories you told

How can different experiences

Make us so similar?

How did the cosmos know we needed each other?

No matter if the laughter roars

Or the tears flow

Together

We are ourselves

That's the safety we offer one another

That's the level of our love

My Friend

The Temptress

She was fire

And I the moth to her flame

Her hair burned red

Waves of amber beauty

To touch her was a sin

The punishment

Eternal hell

Her lips were crimson

And plump

They made my mouth water

I was her Eve

She, my forbidden fruit

My apple

Her beauty was autumn

She glowed with inviting warmth

To resist her

Caused physical pain

I was damned either way

To not hold her in my arms

To not drown in her essence

Would leave me a mere shell

But if I dared to lay myself

At her feet

I would be condemned

Looking at her

Her flame locks

Her daring eyes

I knew I was already damned

For who could ever say no to

The Temptress

That First Kiss

She was angry

Hurt

And her heart ached

For the one she loved

Why didn't he show his true feelings?

Was their friendship so important?

That he'd refuse

What his heart wanted?

Tears stung her eyes

As she took her first steps

Away

From the friend she had come to love

He grabbed her wrist

Spun her around

And just before his mouth

Came crashing down on hers

She saw tears in his eyes

He pulled her into him

Wrapped his arms tight around her

And ravaged her mouth

He was everywhere

He invaded her senses

Right there in the street

In the midst of a downpour

His hands kept pulling her closer

One weaving its way into her hair

He held her

While his tongue worshiped her mouth

Licking into her

Dancing with her own

His lips were hard and demanding

He tilted her head

His teeth caught her bottom lip

And he pulled until she moaned with pleasure

Cars honked as they passed

People stopped and stared

But neither noticed

Both were caught in this moment

This kiss

This claiming of one another

Finally she managed to move

But all she did was try in vain

To get closer to him

Their bodies were pressed so close together

Each could feel the buttons and zips

Of the others clothing pressing into them

It was safe to say

In that kiss

Their friendship was assassinated

But their love and lust for one another

Shone so bright

It made the stars dull in comparison

In That First kiss

Always

I'd walk for miles

To hold you in my arms

Scale the tallest mountains

Swim the deepest seas

I need you to know

You. Are. Loved.

I want you to feel safe

Let's stay up talking

Until the break of dawn

My secrets are yours

Their lock is always open to you

A love built on innocent foundations

A love for the truest of friends

Patchwork Rhythm

No longer steady

No longer strong

The beat is now broken

The rhythm all wrong

Cracked and hurt

Burst at the seams

My heart is all tattered

Tied together with string

A patchwork of love

No longer requited

A cross stitch of tears

Unable to be contained

My hearts on my sleeve

Where it's always been

Open and hurt

Yet still beating

I live in hope

That one day it will mend

Until that day

I entrust it to you

My most valued friend

The Final Curtain

The final curtain draws ever closer

Descending slowly

Allowing one final glance

Before darkness consumes the moon

My howling friend

My mystical lunar

How will my soul carry on without you?

Crushed red velvet obscures my view

Reflections and shadows upon the floor

Offer a moment of peace

As the wolf inside howls one last time

The heavy drapes come silently crashing down

Your final act

Howling At The Fucking Moon

Is my undoing

** In memory of two poets who touched my heart. Gone, but never forgotten Tony & Marcus. May your howls blow on the wind forevermore **

<u>Flash Poetry</u>

To dream

Or

Not to dream

Can never be the question

Acceptance can by mighty

But never

When looking at what you have achieved

While there's air in your chest

There is no full stop

Never accept all which you have done

As all you can do

To dream

Is to live

ABOUT THE AUTHOR

Lisa Fulham is a writer of romantic erotica and poetry. She is the author of *Out on Business,* the poetry anthology *Words of a Soul* and *Delicious Just Desserts.*

She lives in Manchester, England with her family and a dog named Smudge. She loves 80s movies, all things 90s, her friends, and playing in her imagination.

Find her work online at lisafulham298.wordpress.com and follow her on Twitter: @lisa298

Made in the USA
Charleston, SC
07 February 2016